The Grea

Indian Curries

Ever Created!

A Cookbook of 50 Delicious Curry Recipes Direct from India

By

Meera Joshi

More books by Meera Joshi:

Disclaimer

All reasonable efforts have been made to provide accurate and error-free recipes within this book. These recipes are intended for use by persons possessing the appropriate technical skill, at their own discretion and risk. It is advisable that you take full note of the ingredients before mixing and use substitutes where necessary, to fit your dietary requirements.

2

Table of Contents

Introduction

India is a country with unique idiosyncrasies and nuances that can often best be explored by learning about its range of diversity, present in its traditional and contemporary food. It is not uncommon for an Indian native to find another county's food bland in comparison to what they are used to. This is because the Indian palette is doused regularly with spices and curries almost every day. A curry can be defined as a combination of dried spices, fresh herbs and aromatics, blended together, toasted or fried in oil, ghee or butter and mixed with a combination of vegetables, meat or legumes to create a curry-based dish. The differentiating factor that separates one curry from another is the specific combination of spices, herbs and aromatics used in the curry mixture and the way in which the heat is balanced or enhanced. The recipes in this book have won the hearts of many all over the world, originating from the many states of India. As you explore some of the recipes in this book, the contrasting styles between the various regions of India will become apparent, for example the southern India's abundance of coconut trees utilizes all parts of the coconut, in contrast the north, being predominantly an agricultural basin, prefer to use dairy – cream and paneer cheese to balance the curry spices.

The following compilation of recipes are focused on providing a multitude of curry variations from different regions of India. A large number of the Indian population remain vegetarian and rely on lentils or dals to obtain protein and other nutrients, however, a significant number of Indians also eat meat, including beef. Based on this variation, these recipes are organized into sections; the first section provides lentil soups or dal curries from all regions of India, prepared in a way that is unique to that part of India.

The next section of the book focuses on vegetable based curries, vegetables are the hallmark of an Indian meal. Indian curry based vegetables are the centerpiece of a meal, instead of just being offered as a side dish. The meat based curry recipes include the popular Chicken Tikka Masala and the Garlicky Prawns. There is also a section which includes the dishes that accompany curries such as rice and roti. Finally, the book ends with recipes that highlight a handful of the curry masala blends, which are a main component of some of the curry recipes.

Whether you are looking to explore Indian curries in more detail or you are wanting to include more whole grains, vegetables or meat into your meal, this book provides a solid foundation on some of the popular and some not-so-popular curry dishes from all over India. You can also use the recipes as a template to enable you to create and modify dishes to suit your taste and need. These recipes are very adaptable, whether you prefer a vegan or more meat friendly meal. I urge you to be creative as you prepare each dish and most importantly…have fun!

Dal Curries

1. Arhar Dal Curry

This is the most basic and common form of dal curry found among all regions of India. It is a daily staple to most households. The dal remains constant, the tarka and seasoning vary between different regions. This one is popular in the western part of India.

Serves 4

Ingredients:
Dal:
1 cup arhar dal or split-yellow pigeon peas
4 to 5 cups water
½ tsp. turmeric
½ tsp.salt
3-4 pieces dried mangosteen flowers or (Kokum), optional

Tarka or Dal Fry:
3 tbsp ghee or oil of your choice
1 tsp. black mustard seeds
1 medium yellow onion, chopped
5-6 curry leaves
2-inch knob of fresh ginger, grated
3 garlic cloves, finely chopped
Salt, to taste

Method:

1. Prepare the dal by rinsing it in cold running water until washed water appears clear, about 3-4 minutes. Soak the dal in water overnight in the same pot that you prepare to cook. You can reduce the soak time by half if you are strapped with time.
2. Cook the dal by adding turmeric, salt and kokum and bringing it to a boil. Cover the pot and reduce the heat to simmer and cook for approx. 20 to 30 minutes.
3. While the dal is cooking, prepare the tarka by heating a medium sized skillet over medium heat. Add the mustard seeds and wait for about 30 secs to a min for them to sizzle and pop. Add the onions curry leaves, ginger, and garlic to the dal and cook until onions are caramelized for about 10 minutes.
4. Once the dal is fully cooked, add the tarka to it. Adjust salt to taste and serve.

Pairs well with – any variation of flatbreads or with steamed Basmati rice.

2. Moong Dal Smothered in Spinach

Moong Dal has a mellow and creamy taste. Although not a daily staple dal, this dal can be a good gateway 'dal' for someone wanting to get introduced to the complex world of lentils.

Serves 4

Ingredients:
Dal:
1 cup whole moong dal (green in this form)
4 cups water
1 bunch fresh (leaves, rinsed, washed and chopped) or 16 oz. frozen spinach
1 tsp. turmeric
1 tsp. salt

Tarka or Dal Fry:
4 ghee or oil of your choice
1 tsp. cumin seeds
1 tsp coriander powder
1 tsp cumin powder
1 medium yellow onion, chopped
2-inch knob of fresh ginger, grated
4 garlic cloves, finely chopped
1 medium tomato, chopped
Salt, to taste

Method:
1. Rinse and soak the dal for 8-10 hours in a deep stock pot which can be the same used to cook the dal.
2. When ready to cook, add prepared spinach, turmeric and salt. Bring the dal mixture to boil. Cover and reduce the heat to medium low and simmer to cook. Approx. 30 minutes.
3. While the dal is cooking, prepare the tarka by heating up ghee or oil in a skillet over medium-high heat.

4. Add the cumin seeds and wait for 30 seconds for it to start sizzling. Add the coriander and cumin powder and let the spices toast for another 30 seconds.
5. Add the onion and cook for 5 minutes or until translucent.
6. Add the ginger, garlic and cook for 3 more minutes.
7. Add the tomato and cook for additional 5 to 7 minutes.
8. Add the cooked mixture to the cooked spinach and dal mixture and simmer for a few minutes before serving. Adjust salt and seasoning to taste.

Pairs well with – any variation of flatbreads or with steamed Basmati rice.

3. Chayote Squash & Urad Dal Curry

Chayote Squash is also known as Chow Chow in the Southern regions of India. This method of dal preparation is very common in this region in which coconut is regularly used.

Serves 2

Ingredients:
Dal:
1 cup split urad dal
4 cups water
1 chayote squash, pitted and cubed
1 tsp. turmeric
1 tsp. salt

Tarka:
3-4 tbsp.ghee or oil
¼ cup dried shredded coconut
1 tsp yellow pigeon peas or tuvar dal
1 medium onion, cubed
1 tsp mustard seeds
8-10 curry leaves
2 dried Thai chilies
2-inch knob fresh ginger, grated into ginger paste

Method:
1. Rinse and soak the dal for 8-10 hours in a deep stock pot which can be the same used to cook in.
2. When ready to cook, add chayote squash, turmeric and salt. Bring the dal mixture to boil. Cover and reduce the heat to medium low and simmer to cook. Approx. 30 minutes.
3. While the dal is cooking, prepare the tarka by heating up ghee or oil in a skillet over medium-high heat.
4. Add the mustard seeds and tuvar dal. Wait for 30 seconds for it to sizzle and pop.

5. Add the onion and cook for 5 minutes or until translucent.
6. Add the ginger, curry leaf, thai chilies, shredded coconut and cook for 3-5 more minutes.
7. Add the cooked mixture to the cooked dal mixture and simmer for a few minutes before serving. Adjust salt to taste.

Pairs well with - any variation of flatbreads or with steamed Basmati rice.

4. Tangy, Sweet & Spicy Dumplings in Dal (Dal Dhokli)

This lentil soup makes a unique one pot meal hailing from the western part of the country from the state of Gujarat. This soup takes the roti and adds it to the dal instead of having to serve it separately. The result is smooth dumplings floating in the dal mixture. The sweet, tangy and spicy flavors make this dish very addictive.

Ingredients:
Dal:
1 cup split yellow pigeon-peas, picked for stones and rinsed
6-7 cups water
1 tsp salt
1 tsp ground turmeric
3-4 kokum pieces (optional)
2 fresh chilies, stemmed and cut crosswise
1 tsp cumin power
1 tsp coriander powder
1 tbsp jiggery or sugar
1 tbsp tamarind concentrate

Dumplings:
½cup whole wheat flour
1 tbsp chickpea flour (optional)
1 tsp jiggery or sugar
½ tsp salt
½ tsp cayenne pepper
½ tsp ground turmeric
½ tsp ajwain or bishop's weed
1 tbsp oil or ghee
¼ cup water or more as needed

Tarka:
1 tsp cumin seeds
1 tsp mustard seeds
½ tsp fenugreek seeds
8-10 curry leaves
1 bay leaf
1 medium tomato
½ cup chopped onions
2 tbsp finely chopped cilantro

Method:
1) Prepare the dal by soaking it between 4-8 hours in the same pot that will be used to cook the dal.
2) Cook the dal by adding water, kokum, chilies, turmeric and salt. Bring the mixture to boil. Turn the heat to medium, cover and simmer the lentil for 40 minutes or until cooked into soup consistency.
3) While the lentils are cooking, prepare the dumpling dough; in a medium sized mixing bowl combine flour, jaggery, salt, cayenne pepper, turmeric, ajwain and stir to combine. Rub the ghee or oil into the flour. Add enough water to wet the dough into large lumps and bring it together to form a ball, knead a few times ensuring that the final dough shape remains a ball. Set aside while you return to the dal.
4) Check for the doneness of dal. Add the remaining spices – cumin, coriander, jaggery, tamarind to the dal while it continues to simmer. Taste and adjust salt if necessary. Continue to simmer the dal on low heat.
5) Return to the dough; form the dough into 12-inch log and cut cross-wise into ¼ inch circles. Press each circle in between the palm of your hands to flatten. Once all the dough is shaped, add the 'dhokli' or dumplings into the dal that is simmering and cook for 15 -20 minutes.

6) Prepare the tarka by heating oil or ghee in a wide skillet over medium-high heat. Add cumin seeds, mustard seeds and fenugreek seeds, curry leaf and bay leaf and let the spices sizzle. Add the chopped onions and cook over medium heat for 5-8 minutes until translucent and start to caramelize. Add the chopped tomato and continue to cook until softened and the mixture is similar to a sauce.
7) Add the tarka to the dal. Stir to combine and continue to cook on low heat for 5-10 minutes.
8) Garnish with freshly chopped cilantro and serve.

Paris well with – One pot meal, even more enticing the next day as the soup cools and thickens. Enjoy it cold or warmed.

5. Masoor and Moong (Red and Yellow) Dal with Ginger, Garlic and Curry Leaves

This dal combines north Indian ingredients such as ginger, garlic and tomatoes with the staple South Indian ingredient of curry leaves.

Serves 5-6

Ingredients:
Dal:
½cup split and hulled green lentils/moong dal (yellow in this form)
½ cup split and hulled brown lentils/masoor dal (red in this form)
4 cups water
½ tsp turmeric
½ tsp salt

Tarka:
2-inch knob of ginger, grated
4 cloves garlic, finely chopped
2 fresh Thai chilies
2 tsp, ground cumin
1 medium onion, cubed
1 large or 2 medium tomatoes, diced
2 full strands of curry leaves, approximately 30-35
½ tsp turmeric
½ tsp salt
Fresh chopped cilantro for garnish

Method:
1. Prepare the dal by picking over the moong and masoor dal for any stones and rinsing it in cold water. Soak in the water for approximately ½ hour up to 2 hours.

2. Cook the lentils with 4 cups of water. Add turmeric and salt. Bring the lentils to boil over high heat. Reduce the heat, cover the pot and cook until lentils are broken down to soup consistency. Approximately 30 minutes.
3. In the meantime prepare the tarka by first making a paste of cumin powder, ginger, garlic, chilies and curry leaves, then either pound in a pestle and mortar or use a spice grinder. Set aside.
4. Heat a skillet over a medium heat. Add onions and the prepared paste above and cook for about 5 minutes or longer until onions start to caramelize. Add the tomato, salt, turmeric and fresh chopped cilantro. Reduce the heat and cook until tomato pieces are broken down to a saucy consistency.
5. Transfer the mixture into the cooked dal and simmer for a few minutes. Adjust salt to taste.

Pairs well with – any variation of flatbreads or with steamed Basmati rice.

6. Gujarati Buttermilk Curry

This curry is a form of yogurt soup, thickened with chickpea flour. The combination of those two ingredients delivers a high protein content for vegetarians from the Indian state of Gujarat.

Serves 4 persons

Ingredients:
Buttermilk Base:
2 cups plain yogurt or 2 ½ cup buttermilk
5 tbsp chickpea flour
1 tsp kosher salt
2 tsp jaggery
½ tsp ground turmeric

Tarka:
2 tbsp ghee or oil
2 tsp cumin seeds
½ tsp mustard seeds
½ tsp ajwain or bishop's weed
2 tsp ginger, finely chopped
2 tsp garlic, finely chopped
1 tsp fresh thai chili, chopped
12 curry leaves
2 tbsp fresh chopped cilantro

Method:
1. Combine yogurt with 2 cups or if using buttermilk add ½ cup water. Sprinkle with chickpea flour, 1 tbsp at a time and whisk to combine. Then stir salt, jaggery and turmeric and set aside.
2. Make the ginger, garlic and chili paste by pounding in a pestle and mortar, or in a food processor.
3. Heat a skillet over medium-high, add the ghee or oil. Add the cumin seeds and mustard seeds. Wait until the seeds pop.

4. Add ginger, garlic chili paste and the curry leaves and cook for 30 seconds.
5. Add the mixture to the buttermilk mixture and cook over medium to low heat until the soup base is thickened approximately 15-20 minutes.
6. Garnish with cilantro and serve.

Pairs well with – any variation of flatbreads or with steamed Basmati rice.

7. Spicy Dumplings in Buttermilk (Paruppu Unday More Kozhumbu)

Tamil or South Indian variation on the Gujarati Kadhi mentioned above. Here the base is made with buttermilk, it also requires a separate tarka and an extra step of making lentil dumplings. This is a little more effort than the previous buttermilk soup, but worth the effort.

Serves 4 persons

Ingredients:
Dumpling:
1 cup split yellow pigeon peas or tuvar dal, rinsed
3-4 dried red chilies, stems removed
1 tsp salt
2 tsp oil
1 tsp mustard seeds
¼ cup curry leaves
½ cup medium onion
2 tbsp shredded coconut
2 tsp fresh coriander, finely chopped

Curry:
2 ½ cup buttermilk
½ cup shredded dried coconut
1 tbsp cumin seeds
3-4 dried thai chilies
5 tbsp rice flour or chickpea flour

Tarka:
2 tbsp oil of your choice
1 tsp mustard seeds
15-20 curry leaves
2-3 red chilies

Method:

1. Prepare the dumplings; soak the dal along with dried chilies for at least 30 minutes or up to 4 hours.
2. Drain the dal and chilies. Add salt and transfer to a food processor. Process until smooth.
3. Heat a skillet over medium high heat. Add the mustard seeds and after 30 seconds, once they start to pop add curry leaves and onion, then cook for 5-10 minutes.
4. Add the tuvar dal paste and cook for a few minutes. Turn off the heat, fold in the coconut and fresh coriander.
5. Form into medium sized balls and steam them for 10 minutes. Set aside
6. Prepare the curry by whisking the buttermilk with dried coconut and rice flour in a sauce pan.
7. In a food processor make a paste by combining the ½ cup coconut, cumin seeds and Thai chiles into a paste.
8. Add the coconut paste to the buttermilk and bring the mixture to a gentle boil. Turn off the heat and add the dumplings. Be gentle or the dumpling will fall apart.
9. Prepare the tarka by heating up oil in a sauce pan over medium heat add mustard seeds, curry leaves and chilies and cook for 2-3 minutes.
10. Add the tarka to the buttermilk mixture and serve.

Pairs well with – any variation of flatbreads or with steamed Basmati rice.

8. Tomato Rasam or Curry Laced Tomato & Lentil Broth

This is one of the most popular dishes or soups of Madras (Chennai) in southern India. Tomato gives it the tartness but sometimes tamarind, lime or unripe mangos are used to provide the same flavor.

Serves: 6-8 persons

Ingredients:
Dal:
1 pound ripe tomatoes, fresh or canned, finely chopped or processed in a food processor
1/2 cup yellow split pigeon peas or tuvar dal, picked over with stones and washed
2 cups water
1 tsp salt
1 ½ tsp ground cumin
2 tsp ground coriander
1 tsp cayenne
1 tbsp lemon juice

Tarka:
3 tbsp ghee or oil
1 tsp mustard seeds
1 tbsp onion, finely cubed
2-3 cloves garlic, chopped
10-15 curry leaves

Method:
1. Prepare the dal by rinsing it and soaking it for at least 4 hours and up to 8 hours.
2. When ready to make the dal ensure the dal has enough water to measure at least 2 cups, add more if needed.

3. Add tomatoes, salt, cumin, coriander and cayenne. Cook over medium-high heat in a stockpot and bring the mixture to boil. Lower the heat and cook until lentils are cooked well and broken down to a soup consistency.
4. Once the dal is cooked add lemon juice.
5. Prepare the tarka by heating ghee or oil in a skillet over medium heat. Add mustard seeds and wait for 30 seconds to a minute for them to sizzle and pop.
6. Add onion, garlic and curry leaves and cook for a few minutes.
7. Add the mixture into the tomato dal and simmer on low heat for 5 more minutes.
8. Serve while it's still hot.

Pairs well with – typically served on its own or alongside a southern Indian meal.

9. Lemony Moong Bean Broth with Coconut

This is variation of moong dal is prepared with coconut and added tartness provided by fresh lemon juice. It is a common variety of dal curry cooked in various overlapping regions of India.

Serves: 6-8 persons

Ingredients:
Dal:
1/2 cup split moong dal, yellow in this form
5 cups water
½ cup shredded coconut
1 tsp salt
1 tsp ground cumin
½ tsp ground black pepper
2 hot green chilies
1 tbsp lemon juice

Tarka:
3 tbsp ghee or oil
1 tsp mustard seeds
¼ tsp ground asafetida
12 – 15 curry leaves

Method:
1. Prepare the dal by rinsing it and soaking it for a minimum of 30 minutes or up to 2 hours.
2. When ready to cook, ensure there is enough water to cover 4 inches above the dried dal. More water can be added later.

3. Add salt to dal and bring the mixture to boil over high heat. Cover the pot, reduce the heat to low and simmer until dal is cooked. Approximately 20-30 minutes.
4. Once the dal is cooked, add coconut, cumin, black pepper, chilies and lemon juice. Continue to simmer the dal on low heat
5. Prepare the tarka by heating ghee or oil in a skillet over medium heat. Add mustard seeds and wait for 30 seconds to a minute for them to sizzle and pop.
6. Add asafetida and shake the pan for a few seconds and add curry leaves.
7. Add the mixture into the lemony moong dal and simmer on low heat for 5 more minutes.
8. Serve while it's still hot.

Pairs well with – any variation of flatbreads or with steamed basmati rice.

10. Red Lentil Curry with Caramelized Onions

Caramelized onions deliver an unexpected amount of depth of flavor to any dish and dal curries are no exception. This dish is a contemporary take on a masoor dal curry and not specifically related to any region of India.

Dal:
1 cup split brown lentils or masoor dal (red color in this form)
½ tsp salt

Tarka:
1 tsp cumin seeds
½ tsp cardamom seeds
4 piece whole cloves
½ tsp ground black pepper
3 to 4 Thai green chilies
6 tbsp ghee or oil
1 large onion, cut in half and sliced lengthwise
2 medium tomatoes, chopped
½ tsp ground turmeric
2 tbsp freshly chopped cilantro for garnish

Method:
1. Prepare the dal by rinsing it and soaking it for 30 minutes or up to 2 hours.
2. When ready to cook, ensure the dal has enough water to cover 4 inches above the dried dal. More water can be added later.
3. Add salt to dal and bring the mixture to boil over high heat. Cover the pot, reduce the heat to low and simmer until dal is cooked. Approximately 20-30 minutes.

4. Once the dal is cooked, prepare for the tarka; in a small skillet roast cumin seeds, cardamom seeds, cloves, black peppers over low heat. Turn off the heat and let it cool. In a food processor combine the roasted spices with chilies and pulverize to a paste. Set aside.
5. Heat a medium skillet over medium-high heat, add the ghee and heat for a few minutes. Add onions and the chili/spice pulverized paste and cook for 10-15 minutes. Adjust heat as necessary.
6. Add tomatoes, turmeric and pinch of salt to the mixture and cook over medium heat for 10 more minutes.
7. Add the mixture into the dal mixture and simmer on low heat for 5 more minutes.
8. Serve while it's still hot.

Pairs well with – any variation of flatbreads or with steamed Basmati rice.

11.   Spicy Black-Eyed Beans with Swiss Chard

Black eyed beans are not prepared as often as the dal curries. They are saved for a special occasion, this perhaps could be due to the additional step of having to soak the black-eyed peas over night before cooking it. Whatever the reason, this way of preparing them will make you wonder why it is not made more often. You can substitute spinach instead of swiss chard if you like.

Dal:
2 cups black eyed peas
½ tsp salt
2 tsp coriander powder
½ stick or 1 small stick of cinnamon
1 tsp turmeric
3 serrano peppers, chopped
1 bunch of fresh swiss chards, stems removed and chopped separately and leaves sliced thinly

Tarka:
3 tbsp ghee or oil
2 tsp cumin seeds
1 tsp garam masala
1 small onion, chopped into cubes
4-5 cloves garlic
½ tsp asafetida powder
Salt to taste

Method:

1. Prepare by rinsing and soaking the black-eyed peas overnight in water.
2. When ready to cook, ensure the dal has enough water to cover 6 inches above the beans. More water can be added later.
3. Add salt to the beans and bring the mixture to boil over high heat. Cover the pot, reduce the heat to low and simmer until dal is cooked. Approximately 60 minutes
4. Once the beans are cooked add salt, coriander powder, cinnamon and chilies.
5. Prepare for the tarka. Heat a medium skillet over medium-high heat, add the ghee and heat for a few minutes. Add the cumin seeds and let it sizzle for a few minutes. Once the skillet and oil is hot, add onions, and garlic along with asafetida. Add the swiss chard stems and continue to cook over medium-high heat until onions are caramelized.
6. Add the onion mixture to the pot of beans and stir to combine and continue to simmer.
7. Add the swiss chard leaves along with the garam masala and continue to simmer for 5 -10 minutes.
8. Add salt to taste.

Pairs well with – any variation of flatbreads or with steamed Basmati rice.

12. Toasted Moong Dal with Spinach

This is a Bengali way of making lentils, which is to toast or roast them first. The resulting dal here is less soupy than the ones commonly associated with making moong dal.

Dal:
1 cup split moong dal (yellow in this form), picked over for stones
½ tsp turmeric powder
1 tsp coriander powder
1 tsp cumin powder
1 ½ tsp salt
2 tsp jaggery or sugar

½ lb fresh spinach or 4 oz frozen spinach

Tarka:
2 tbsp ghee or oil
1 bay leaf
2-inch knob of ginger
3-4 garlic, minced
2 to 4 dried red Thai chilies or fresh serrano chilies
Salt to taste

Method:
1. Prepare the dal; heat medium sized saucepan over medium-high heat, add moong dal and toast stirring constantly for 5 to 8 minutes or until it appears reddish in color and starts smelling nutty.

2. With the pan still on the stove's flame, pour 3 cups of water into the pan. Stir to breakup any lumps that may form. Be careful as the water will sizzle and start boiling fairly quickly.
3. Add turmeric salt, cumin, coriander powder and sugar. Stir to combine.
4. Reduce the heat, cover the lentils and cook until tender, approximately 15-20 minutes.
5. When the lentils are close to being done, add the spinach and cook over low heat until wilted.
6. Prepare for the tarka. Heat a medium skillet over medium-high heat, add the ghee and heat for a few minutes. Add the bay leaf, ginger, garlic and red chilies. Cook for 30 seconds or until it sizzles.
7. Add the tarka back to the pan and continue to cook for a few more minutes.
8. Taste and adjust salt to taste. Serve with naan or rice

Pairs well with – any variation of flatbreads or with steamed Basmati rice.

13. Cashew Nut Curry (Kaju Curry)

A curry made mostly of nuts is a specialty hailing from Sri Lanka. The combination of cinnamon, cardamom and bay leaf lends itself to a naturally sweet and creamy combination that is pleasing to the palatte, body and soul.

Serves 4

Ingredients:
1 can unsweetened coconut milk
2 cups cashew nuts
½ cup fresh or frozen green peas
¼ cup fresh or frozen corn kernels
1 medium sweet potato, scrubbed, peeled and cubed
1 tsp salt or to taste
½ tsp ground turmeric
6 cardamom pods
6 whole cloves
1 to 2 cinnamon sticks
½ tsp cayenne

3 tbsp ghee or oil
½ cup onion, cubed
3-4 cloves garlic, minced

Method:
1) Place the cashews in a medium sized saucepan add water and cover. Bring to a rolling boil over high heat. Remove the pan from the heat. Cover and set aside for cashews to soften, about 2 hours.
2) Drain and return the cashews to the same saucepan. Add coconut milk, green peas, corn and sweet potato, salt, turmeric, cayenne, cardamom pods, whole cloves, cinnamon sticks and bring to boil. Reduce the heat and simmer.
3) Make the tarka by heating ghee or oil in a small skillet over medium-high heat, add onions, garlic and curry leaves. Cook for 30 seconds to a minute and remove from the heat.
4) Combine the tarka with the cashews and serve.

Pairs well with – any variation of flatbreads or with steamed Basmati rice.

Vegetable Curries

14. Navratan Korma (Vegetables with Cashews & Raisin)

A special occasion curry which emanates the royal palaces' kitchens in Moghul India.

Serves 4

Ingredients:
½ cup frozen or fresh green beans
½ cup cauliflower florets
¼ cup fresh or frozen green peas
½ cup bottle gourd squash
1 small carrot, peeled, trimmed, cut into cubes
1 small potato, Yukon gold, rinsed and cubed
1 sweet potato, rinsed and cubed
1 small green or red bell pepper
½ tsp salt

4 oz paneer or tofu, cut into ½ inch cubes and pan-fried

Cashew-Raisin Sauce:
4 tbsp ghee or oil
1 medium onion, cubed
1 small tomato, diced
½ cup cashews
¼ cup raisins
2-inch knob of fresh ginger, grated

4-5 cloves, smashed
3-4 tsp whole cloves
2-3 cardamom seeds
1 to 2 dried of fresh bay leaves
½ turmeric
1 tsp ground cumin
1 tsp ground coriander
½ tsp cinnamon
¼ tsp black pepper ground
Fresh cilantro for garnish

Method:
1) Combine the green beans, cauliflower, peas, squash, carrot, potatoes and bell-pepper in a medium-sized sauce pan. Add enough water to cover 1-inch over the vegetables. Place on medium-high heat and bring the mixture to boil. Lower the heat and continue to simmer until the vegetables are cooked. Approximately 7-10 minutes.
2) Reserve 2 cups of liquid by draining the cooked vegetables. Return the vegetables in the saucepan and set aside.
3) Prepare the Cashew-Raisin sauce; heat the ghee in a wide skillet over medium-high heat. Add the onions, tomatoes, cashews, raisins, ginger, garlic, cloves, cardamom seeds and bay leaves. Cook stirring occasionally until the onions are caramelized and nuts are browned. Approximately 15 minutes. Pour ½ cup of reserved water to deglaze the mixture and release the browned bits.
4) Cool the mixture and transfer to a food processor and blend well. Add the remaining spices: turmeric, cumin, coriander, black pepper, cinnamon and puree to mix.
5) Add this sauce to the vegetables in the sauce pan.
6) Pour the remaining 1 ½ cups of water.

7) Add the paneer to the vegetables and sauce mixture. Turn on the stove to medium-high heat and bring the mixture to boil and lower the heat to simmer for 10 minutes.

8) Garnish with cilantro and serve with naan or rice.

Pairs well with – any variation of flatbreads or with steamed Basmati rice.

15.   Saag Paneer (Indian Cheese in Fragrant Spinach Sauce)

For the Indians living in the north, Indian cheese is a delicacy saved for special occasions. This recipe is cooked in an onion-cumin-fenugreek-laced spinach sauce.

Serves 4

Ingredients:
8-oz Paneer Indian Cheese, cubed
1 lb fresh spinach or 8 oz frozen spinach
1 tbsp dried fengugreek leaves
5 tbsp ghee or oil
2 tsp cumin
1 medium onion, chopped
2-inch knob of fresh ginger, grated or diced finely
1 tsp turmeric
2 hot green chilies such as serrano or jalapeno, minced
1 tsp salt or to taste
2 tsp garam masala

Method:
1. Saute the paneer in a skillet by heating 2 tbsp of oil or ghee over medium-high heat. Add the paneer cubes and sauté until golden brown in color and set aside.
2. Cook the spinach by blanching it in hot boiling water for 2-3 minutes. Drain and set aside.
3. Make the sauce by heating 4 tbsp of oil in a large pan over medium-high heat. Add the cumin seeds and wait for it to sizzle. Add the onions and ginger. Cook by stirring frequently for 2 minutes. Add the turmeric, chilies and stir to cook for a few seconds.

4. Add the Spinach and fenugreek puree to the sauce along with 1 cup water, add salt. Raise the heat and bring the mixture to boil. Lower the heat and continue to simmer.
5. Add the paneer slices and garam masala. Continue to simmer for a few more minutes. Taste, then adjust the salt to taste.
6. Serve hot.

Pairs well with - any variation of flatbreads or with steamed Basmati rice.

16.   Mullingatawny

This soup has its roots from the Southern part of India where in Tamil, the name means peppered water. Since the colonial period, the soup evolved into a creamy (from coconut) variation and the British even added meat to it.

Serves: Makes 12 to 16 naan

Ingredients:
1 cup red lentils or masoor dal
3 tbsp butter, ghee or oil
1 tsp black mustard seeds
1 medium onion, cubed
1 medium tomato, chopped
1 medium-sized green, yellow or orange bell pepper, stemmed, seeded and cut into cubes
1 large carrot, peeled, finely chopped
6 cloves garlic, minced
1 small head cauliflower, rinsed and cubed into medium-sized florets
1 ½ tsp salt
1 tsp cumin powder
1 ½ tsp coriander powder
½ tsp cardamom ground
1 tsp turmeric
1 tsp black pepper
1 tsp cayenne
1 cup coconut milk
1 cup frozen or fresh green peas

Method:
1) Prepare the dal by rinsing and soaking it for a few hours. Add enough water to cover 4 inches above the dal and bring the mixture to boil over high heat. Cover and reduce the heat to cook the lentils. Approximately 30 minutes. Set aside to cool.

2) In a wide skillet heat the ghee, butter or oil. Add the mustard seeds, cover the pan and cook until the seeds pop. Add the onion, tomato, bell peppers, carrots and garlic.

3) Cook until onions are golden-brown or caramelized. Add the cauliflower. Sprinkle with salt, cumin powder, coriander powder, cardamom, turmeric, pepper, and cayenne. Continue to cook over medium high-heat for about 5 to 10 minutes

4) Pour 3 cups of water and bring the mixture to boil over high heat. Reduce the heat to low and continue to simmer for 10 to 15 minutes.

5) Meanwhile, transfer the cooked lentils along with their cooking water to a blender and pulse on high to puree until smooth.

6) Add the lentil puree to the vegetable mixture. Bring the mixture to boil. Add the coconut milk and peas and continue to simmer for 10 more minutes.

Pairs well with - any variation of flatbreads or with steamed Basmati rice.

17. Bottle Gourd Squash Laced in Fenugreek Sauce

Bottle gourd squash is a green hued squash that is shaped like a cylindrical long bottle, which is known to be used in a milk based dessert and also commonly used to make curry with split yellow peas. However, here it is cooked on its own and flavored with fenugreek. This recipe is simple and quick to put together

Serves 4-6

Ingredients:
1 medium sized bottle gourd squash
3-4 tbsp butter, ghee or oil
1 bunch of fresh or 1 14 oz bag of frozen fenugreek leaves
1 large tomato, cut into cubes
½ tsp ground turmeric
1 ½ tsp salt
½ tsp cayenne or ground red pepper

Method:
1) Prepare the squash by first cutting off the stems and peeling the outer tough skin. Cut the squash half in lengthwise. Now cut the squash into 1 inch pieces.
2) Place the squash in a bowl and toss with turmeric to cover and set aside.
3) In a large skillet, heat the ghee, butter or oil over medium-high heat and add the squash to stir fry for 1 to 2 minutes.
4) Add fenugreek leaves, tomato, salt and cayenne. Stir once or twice.
5) Reduce the heat to medium low, cover the skillet and cook until the squash is tender. Approximately 20-25 minutes.

Pairs well with – any variation of flatbreads or with steamed Basmati rice.

18. Sambharo (Warm Carrot Salad)

This is another easy stir-fry vegetable recipe hailing from the western part of India from the state of Gujarat. It uses mustard seed to flavor and chilies to add the heat. The recipe here doesn't use chilies, but feel free to add sliced ones You can also use cabbage instead of carrots to make it in a similar manner.

Serves 4-6

Ingredients:
3 to 4 (2 cups) medium sized carrots, shredded
2 tbsp oil, butter or ghee
½ tsp mustard seeds
1 tbsp sesame seeds
2 tbsp dried shredded coconut
Pinch asafetida
¾ tsp turmeric
1 tsp salt or to taste
1-2 tsp lemon juice

Method:
1) Prepare the carrots by rinsing them and shredding them. Measure 2 cups and set aside.
2) Heat oil, ghee or butter in a large skillet over medium-high heat. Add the mustard seeds. Wait 30 seconds for it to sizzle and then add sesame seeds, dried shredded coconut and asafetida.

3) Add the shredded carrots and stir to combine the spices. Sprinkle with turmeric and salt. Lower the heat and continue to cook for 5 to 10 minutes or until carrots are tender.
4) Taste and adjust the salt and add lemon juice.

Pairs well with – any variation of flatbreads or with steamed Basmati rice.

19.   Curry Spiced Avocado

Avocados are largely unavailable in northern parts of India, but they are found in abundance in the Southern part of India and especially the Malabar region. The Arabian settlers in the region loved the avocado and found a way to include it into a spice laced salad.

Serves 4 - 8

Ingredients:
1 large ripe avocado
3-4 tbsp fresh lemon juice
¼ cup chopped fresh coriander
8-10 fresh curry leaves
1 tsp salt or to taste

Tarka:
1 tbsp coconut oil
1 tsp black mustard seeds
2-3 cloves garlic, minced
½ cup chopped onion
½ tsp ground coriander
½ tsp ground cumin
¼ tsp ground black pepper
2 green chilies, minced

Method:
1. Cut the avocado in half. Remove the deed and scoop out the pulp. Chop roughly. Stir in the lemon juice, coriander, curry leaves and salt. Set aside.
2. Heat oil in a medium-sized skillet. When hot, add the mustard seeds and cover the pot. When the splattering stops, add the garlic, onion and let it sizzle for 10-15 seconds.

3. Sprinkle the cumin, coriander, black pepper and chilies and cook until onions are translucent and slightly caramelized.
4. Add the avocado mixture. Turn off the heat.
5. Taste and adjust the salt to your liking.

Pairs well with – any variation of flatbreads or with steamed Basmati rice.

20. Bharela Ringan (Aubergines Cooked in Gram Flour Peanut Sauce)

Baby eggplants are known as aubergines. The Gujarati's have a unique way of cooking the eggplant by creating a sauce with a combination of gram flour, coconut and peanuts, filling them in the slit cuts of eggplants and then steaming until tender.

Serves: 4

Ingredients:
12 Baby aubergines
½ cup shredded dried coconut
4 tbsp ground chickpea flour
¾ cup roasted unsalted peanuts, ground
3 tbsp fresh coriander chopped
8-10 cloves garlic, minced
1 green chili
1 medium tomato, cubed
1 tsp ground cumin
¾ tsp ground turmeric
1 ½ - 2 tsp salt
1 tsp sugar
3 tbsp oil of your choice
1 large onion, sliced

Method:
1. Prepare the eggplants by cutting in half lengthways, keeping the stem intact. Roll one over and cut lengthways again, still keeping the stem intact. Put into a bowl of cold water and set aside.
2. Heat a medium-sized skillet over medium heat and when hot, add the coconut, peanuts and gram flour. Roast until fragrant and appear golden brown in color. Transfer to a bowl and let it cool.

3. Put the coriander, garlic, chili, tomato, cumin, turmeric, sugar and salt into food processor. Add the cooled coconut, peanut and gram flour mixture to it. Pulse until coarsely ground and fully mixed.
4. Open each aubergine out and fill with the coconut, peanut mixture using your hands. Repeat this process for the remaining aubergines and set aside.
5. Heat the oil in the skillet over medium-high heat. When hot add onions and fry until golden brown and soft. Add the aubergines and any leftover coconut, peanut mixture. Do not stir the aubergines. Add 2 tbsp of water let the mixture come to a gentle simmer. Cover and lower the heat. Cook until aubergines are tender approximately 20 minutes.

Pairs well with – any variation of flatbreads or with steamed Basmati rice.

21.   Spiced and Curried Potatoes

A southern Indian way of making potatoes, which is one of the simplest form of making curried potatoes. All you need to do is boil potatoes and add a generous amount of curry powder.

Serves 4-6 people

Ingredients:
3-4 tsp oil of your choice
6-10 medium sized Yukon gold potatoes
½ tsp ground cumin
½ tsp ground coriander
¼ tsp ground turmeric
¼ tsp ground black pepper
½ tsp cayenne
1 ½ tsp salt

Method:
1) In a medium saucepan boil the potatoes with their skin on with enough water to cover until tender but still firm. Drain and let it cool for a few minutes. Peel the potatoes.
2) Cut the potatoes in 1 ½ inch thick slices. Sprinkle with cumin, coriander, turmeric and black pepper.
3) Sprinkle 3 to 4 tbsp water over them and toss carefully to coat with spices. Set aside to cool for 15 minutes.
4) Heat the oil in a large skillet over high heat. Once hot, add the potatoes and sprinkle with salt to taste. Reduce heat to medium and fry the potatoes, turning them until golden brown. Approximately 12 -15 minutes.
5) Serve warm or at room temperature.

Pairs well with – any variation of flatbreads or with steamed Basmati rice.

22.　Cabbage Thoran

This quick stir-fry recipe comes from Kerala and whose cuisine is known for its quick stir fries. This is very similar to the Carrot Sambharo recipe, which is from the northern regions of India. Kerala cuisine is known for using coconut oil, curry leaves and mustard seeds. This dish is versatile in the sense that you can use red or green cabbage, carrots, okra or zucchini to make it.

Serves 4-6 people

Ingredients:
4 tbsp coconut oil
1 tsp brown mustard seeds
1 tsp cumin seeds
10-15 curry leaves
1 red cabbage, cored and coarsely chopped
½ cup grated coconut, fresh or dried
½ tsp ground turmeric

½ tsp kosher salt
4-5 garlic cloves, minced
1 serrano chili, thinly sliced lengthwise

Method:
1) In a wide skillet heat the oil over medium-high heat. Add the mustard seeds. Twirl the pan a bit to spread and cover the lid to allow them to pop for 30 seconds.
2) Add the cumin seeds, garlic, curry leaves and cook until fragrant, approximately 30 seconds to a minute.
3) Add cabbage to the pan. Stir to coat the spices. Add turmeric and salt.
4) Cook the cabbage by stirring it frequently, approximately 3 to 5 minutes.
5) Add ½ cup of water and continue to cook the cabbage on medium-high heat for 6-8 minutes.
6) Add the coconut, chilies and ¼ cup of water and cook for additional 2 minutes.
7) The cabbage will be tender, but still a bit crisp and somewhat crunchy.

Pairs well with – Cardamom smothered pork chop

23.   Egg Bhurji

Common amongst college students living dorms away from their families, this is a variation on scrambled eggs.

Serves 4

Ingredients:
6 large eggs
4 tbsp whole milk
2 tbsp oil of your choice
½ tsp ajwain or carom seeds
½ tsp turmeric
½ cup onion, chopped
½ bell pepper, cored, seeded and chopped into ½ inch cubes
1 tomato, chopped
1 ½ tsp salt

Method:
1) Prepare the eggs by cracking them in a bowl. Add milk. Whisk to combine until frothy. Set aside.
2) In a large skillet, heat the oil over medium-high heat. Add the ajwain and wait for 30 seconds.
3) Add the onions, bell pepper and tomato. Stir to combine and cook for 2-3 minutes.
4) Add turmeric and salt and stir to blend the spices evenly to the mixture. Cook for 2 more minutes.
5) Lower the heat and add eggs. Stir to combine the eggs and curdle the mixture. Increase the heat and stir vigorously to cook the mixture.
6) Continue to cook until the eggs are fully cooked. Serve warm.

Pairs well with – Masala Chai and flat bread on the side.

24. Green Pea Soup (Matar Ka Shorba)

This is another contemporary way of preparing dal curry using fresh or frozen peas. The more common variations use the whole dried green peas.

Serves 4-6 people

Ingredients:
2 cups Green Peas (Fresh or frozen)
3-4 tsp ghee or oil
1 medium red onion, finely chopped
4 cloves garlic, minced
2-inch piece ginger
1 tbsp mint, chopped
2 tbsp cilantro, chopped
½ tsp cumin seeds
2 Bay leaves or 4-5 curry leaves
1 cardamom pod, crushed
1 stick cinnamon
Cilantro to granish
Salt to taste

Method:
1) In a medium saucepan bring water to boil over high heat. Also, prepare a bowl of ice-water to dunk the peas into.
2) Only when the water is boiling, add the peas and let it boil for 5-minutes or until tender. Drain and dunk into cold water. Drain and puree in food processor until smooth.
3) In a medium skillet, heat the ghee, butter or oil over medium high heat. Once heated, add the cumin seeds, bay leaves or curry leaves, cardamom, and cinnamon.
4) Add onions and stir to coat the spices. Continue to cook for several minutes.

5) Add garlic, ginger, mint and cilantro and stir to combine. Continue to cook for about 2-3 minutes.
6) Lower the heat and add the peas puree and water as necessary to dilute to your preferred consistency.
7) Taste and adjust to your desired consistency.

Pairs well with – good on its own or any variation of flatbreads or with steamed Basmati rice.

25.   Kohlrabi Smothered in Kohlrabi Greens

This type of preparation applies to kohlrabi, but it can also apply to beets, beet greens and also cauliflower with cauliflower greens. This recipe calls for peanut oil reminiscent of the central region of India scented with cumin, mustard and fenugreek seeds.

Serves 4

Ingredients:
4 to 5 Kohlrabi with Kohlrabi green attached
4 tbsp peanut oil
1 tsp black mustard seeds
1 tsp cumin seeds
1 tbsp ground coriander
½ tsp turmeric
¼ tsp fenugreek
½ tsp cayenne
1 medium onion, finely cubed
1 2-nch knob of fresh ginger, grated
1 tsp salt, or to taste

Method:
1) Prepare the Kohlrabi – rinse kohlrabi along with its greens. Remove the greens and chop them thinly. Set aside. Peel the Kohlrabi bulb and cut into small cubes.
2) Heat a large skillet over medium-high heat. Add oil and wait for it to get heated. Once hot, add the mustard seeds, cover the pan with a lid as they will pop once heated. The popping will subside after 30 seconds.
3) At this point add coriander, fenugreek, turmeric and pepper. Add the chopped onion and continue to stir constantly until caramelized, approx. 6-8 minutes.
4) Add the ginger paste and toast with the onion and spice mixture for 30 seconds.

5) Add the kohlrabi, along with its greens and stir to combine. Cover and cook until tender. Approx. 20 minutes.
6) Continue to check by stirring frequently. Once tender add the salt. Taste and tweak the spices or salt to your liking.
7) Serve warm or at room temperature or cold.

Pairs well with – any variation of flatbreads or with steamed Basmati rice.

26.   Curried Eggplant & Potatoes (Aloo Baigan)

This style of cooking is popular amongst the eastern extremities of the northern states of India, especially those bordering Nepal. This style requires the vegetables to be marinated into the spices and then fried with some oil to develop the roasted flavor.

Serves 4

Ingredients:
1 lb eggplants, Japanese long ones or small aubergines will work as well
1 lb Yukon gold potatoes
½ tsp turmeric
2 tbsp ground coriander
1 tsp cayenne
1 ½ tsp coarse salt
5 tbsp oil of your choice (peanut or mustard oil would make excellent choices)
1 tsp fenugreek seeds
1 ½ tsp mango or amchur powder

Method:
1) Prepare the eggplants and potatoes by rinsing them in cold water. If using organic, feel free to keep the peel intact from both vegetables.
2) Sprinkle with turmeric, coriander, cayenne and salt. Mix well to coat evenly. Set aside.
3) Heat the oil in a large skillet (with a lid) over high heat. Wait for 2-3 minutes for the oil to get completely hot. Add fenugreek seeds and let them cook for 10-15 seconds.
4) Add the vegetables and swirl the pan a few times to spread. Let the vegetables sit and cook in the oil undisturbed for 2 to 3 minutes. Then turn it again and wait for 5 minutes.

5) Once the vegetables appear to have started the cooking process, lower the heat. Cover the skillet and cook for 20 minutes, keeping an eye and turning them often.
6) Once cooked, sprinkle the mango powder. Stir and continue to cook for 5 minutes.
7) Serve warm or at room temperature

Pairs well with – any variation of flatbreads or with steamed Basmati rice.

Meat-Based Curries

27.   Chicken Balti

A popular recipe from Indian cuisine which has become very popular in the United Kingdom. This dish is popular amongst the northwestern states and receives its name from the style of serving dish used– 'Balti', a stainless-steel bowl. This dish is spicy and creamy. The tomato here is added at the end to keep the fresh tart flavor intact, instead of having it cooked down into a sauce.

Serves 8 people

Ingredients:
4 tbsp oil of your choice
1 large green, red or orange bell pepper, stemmed, seeded and cut into 1-inch cubes
1 small red onion, cut into cubes
4 large garlic cloves, thinly sliced
5-6 dried Thai chilies or serrano chilies or any chili substitute you can find with comparable heat, sliced thinly lengthwise
2 – lb boneless, skinless chick breasts, cut into 1-inch pieces
2 tsp Balti masala
½ - ¾ cup full-fat yogurt
¼ cup heavy cream
½ bunch of fresh cilantro, chopped finely
1 large tomato, cored and cut into fine cubes

Method:
1) Heat a wok, or a wide-bottomed saucepan over medium-high heat. Drizzle the oil onto it.
2) When the oil is simmering, add the bell peppers, onion, garlic and chilies. Stir fry until the vegetables appear to be caramelized, 8 to 10 minutes.

3) Add chicken cubes to it and continue to stir-fry until meat is seared, 5-8 minutes.
4) Add cilantro and Balti masala. Stir-fry to cook the spice taking care that it doesn't get burnt.
5) Reduce the heat and continue to cook, stirring occasionally, uncovered. Cook until chicken is a bit tender and no longer pink, 15 minutes.
6) In a separate bowl, combine yogurt with cream. Return back to the chicken, stir and lower the heat. Add yogurt/cream mixture gently to the chicken mixture.
7) Garnish with tomatoes and serve.

Pairs well with – any variation of flatbreads or with steamed Basmati rice.

28. Poached Fish Fillets in Tomato Sauce

It's Bengalis and the South Indians from Kerala who seem to equally share this love affair with cooking and serving fish in curry sauce. Here's a fish curry variation served with a tangy tomato sauce.

Serves 4

Ingredients:
¼ cup coconut oil
1 cup thinly sliced shallots
6 lengthwise slices fresh ginger, julienned into thin stripes
4 large cloves garlic, cut into thin slivers
12 to 15 fresh curry leaves
4 to 5 green chilies, cut into thin slices
2 large tomatoes, cored and cubed
¼ cup distilled white vinegar
1 ½ tsp ground red pepper such as cayenne or paprika
1 ½ tsp kosher salt or to taste
1 ½ lbs skinless fillets with the fish of your choice such as (halibut, salmon or similar)

Method:
1) In a large skillet, heat the oil over medium high heat. Add the shallots, ginger and garlic and cook, stirring the vegetables until golden brown and caramelized, 8-10 minutes.
2) Stir in the curry leaves and fresh chilies and cook stirring for 30 seconds. Then add the tomatoes, vinegar, ground chiles and salt. Lower the heat and continue to cook uncovered, stirring occasionally, until the tomatoes start to break down 4-5 minutes.
3) Add the fish fillets and spoon the sauce over to cover them. Cover the skillet and cook for 10 to 15 minutes.
4) Serve warm.

Pairs well with – any variation of flatbreads or with steamed Basmati rice.

29.   Chicken Tikka Masala

This is another popular Indian dish internationally, especially in the United Kingdom, where it is considered its national dish. This recipe makes good use of the masalas, chili blend and creamy sauce, and the end result is superior to what they serve in average restaurants. This recipe is reminiscent of a rich, delicate dish from the Indian mogul times. It's a two part process in which you marinate the meat first on skewers and cook it, then cook it once again in its sauce.

Serves 4

Ingredients:

Chicken tikkas:
Bamboo or metal skewers
¾ cup plain, full-fat yogurt
3-4-inch ginger, peeled and cut into chunks
3 cloves of garlic cut into chunks
4 tbsp fresh chopped cilantro
2 tsp coriander powder
1 tsp cumin powder
2 tsp ground Kashmiri chilies
1 ½ tsp kosher salt
½ tsp Punjabi garam masala

½ tsp turmeric, ground
1 ½ lb boneless, skinless chicken breasts cut into medium cubes

For the sauce:
2 tbsp ghee, butter or oil of your choice
1 small yellow or red onion, coarsely chopped
1 small red bell pepper, stemmed, seeded and cubed
¼ cup slivered blanched almonds
¼ cup golden raisins
2 medium tomatoes, diced
¼ cup heavy cream or half-and-half
4 tbsp plain, full-fat yogurt
½ tsp coarse kosher salt
¼ tsp cayenne
¼ tsp Punjabi garam masala
Cilantro, chopped

Method:
1) Prepare the chicken tikka marinade by first making a paste out of the garlic, ginger, cilantro and chilies by either mashing them using a pestle and mortar with some salt into a paste or using a food processor. In a medium sized bowl, combine the yogurt, ginger and garlic paste, coriander, cumin, salt, garam masala, and turmeric into a small bowl. Whisk to blend.
2) Add the chicken cubes to the sauce and using your hands, toss to combine and ensure that the sauce covers the chicken. Next, cover the chicken and refrigerate for 2 hours or overnight, recommended in order to marinate.
3) Next day, when ready to cook, prepare the sauce by heating the ghee, oil or butter in a medium sized saucepan. Add the onions, bell peppers, almonds and raisins to the pan, cook stirring frequently until the onions are caramelized, 12-15 minutes.
4) If using a grill, ensure it is prepared and ready to go. Alternately you can cook the chicken in the oven at 425 F. Ensue the oven is pre-heated first.

5) Stir the tomatoes into the pan and stir to deglaze any caramelized vegetables. Cook for 2 to 5 minutes.
6) Remove from the heat. Add the cream, yogurt, salt, cayenne and garam masala. Stir to combine. Let the mixture cool. Puree in a food processor. Return the sauce back to its sauce pan.
7) Grill the chicken or if using oven, line the chicken skewers and place in the oven. Check every 8-10 minutes for doneness and to turn the skewers to ensure all sides are cooked well.

Pairs well with – any variation of flatbreads or with steamed Basmati rice.

30.   Salmon Curried and Roasted

Indian food generally relies on stove top cooking, this recipe requires baking the salmon in the oven, although you can cook it on the stovetop as well.

Serves 4-6 people

Ingredients:
2 tbsp butter, ghee or oil of your choice
1 lb salmon fillet
1 tsp turmeric, ground
4-5 garlic cloves, crushed
½ tsp ground black pepper
½ tsp cayenne
1 ½ tsp salt

Method:
1) Preheat oven to 375 F.
2) Place an aluminum foil over a baking sheet.
3) Place the salmon over it.
4) Heat a small skillet over medium to low heat. Add the butter, ghee or oil to it. Fry the garlic, and add the turmeric, black pepper, cayenne.
5) Add the heated mixture over the salmon.
6) Create a tent with the foil over the salmon and place in the oven.
7) Bake for 25-30 minutes. Remove from the oven and serve.

Pairs well with – Wonderful on its own or with steamed Basmati rice

31.   Garlicky Prawn Pan Roasted

Shrimp are known as prawns in India. This seafood dish is prominent and popular among the coast of Malabar especially Goa and Kerala, where there is a local fishing community.

Serves 4-6 people

Ingredients:
1 lb large shrimp, peeled and deveined with tails on
½ tsp ground turmeric
1 tsp cayenne or hot paprika
6-7 garlic cloves, coarsely chopped or smashed
4 tbsp dried unsweetened coconut, reconstituted
2 tbsp sesame seeds
1 medium tomato, coarsely chopped
3 tbsp oil of your choice
1 tsp salt or to taste
Fresh cilantro, rinsed and chopped for garnish

Method:
1) In a medium sized bowl, toss the shrimp with the turmeric and cayenne or hot paprika. Set aside for approximately 15-20 minutes to absorb the flavors.
2) Make a paste of garlic, coconut, and sesame seeds, either by using a pestle and mortar, or a food processor.
3) In a large skillet, heat the oil over medium-high heat. Once oil is hot, add the coconut paste and cook for 2 to 3 minutes.
4) Add the tomatoes and sprinkle with salt. Cook for 3 to 4 minutes until tomatoes start releasing juice and the mixture appears saucy.
5) Add the marinated shrimp to the mixture and cook uncovered stirring occasionally for 5 to 7 minutes until the shrimp is cooked through.
6) Taste and adjust salt. Garnish with fresh chopped cilantro and serve.

Pairs well with – Part of the main course with rice or any variation of Indian flatbread.

32.   Rogan Josh

Rogan Josh is a lamb dish introduced to India by the Moguls. It is considered to be a traditional dish of the Kashmiri or North Western part of India. It displays the region's flavors and ingredients that are native to the region such as Kashmiri chilies.

Serves 6 people

Ingredients:
¼ cup Greek yogurt or plain yogurt strained overnight
6-8 garlic cloves, peeled and crushed into a paste like consistency
2-3 inch ginger, peeled and smashed into paste like consistency in mortar pestle or food processor
2 tsp Bin bhuna hua garam masala or garam masala of your choice
2 tsp salt, or to taste
1 ½ lb of boneless leg of lamb, fat trimmed and discarded, cut into 1-inch cubes

For Frying:
2-3tbsp butter, ghee or oil of your choice
1 tsp cumin seeds
1 tsp fennel seeds
10-12 whole cloves
4 black or green cardamom pods
8-10 curry leaves or 2 fresh or dried bay leaves

2 cinnamon sticks
1 medium onion, finely chopped
1 medium tomato, cubed
1tbsp Kashmiri chilies or a combination of ¼ tbsp cayenne mixed with
½ tbsp sweet paprika

Method:
1) Whisk the yogurt together with ginger and garlic paste along with garam masala and salt together in a medium-sized bowl. Add the lamb and stir to coat with the marinade. Cover and refrigerate for several hours or overnight.
2) On the day of cooking, heat ghee, butter or oil over a wide-skillet over medium heat. Sprinkle with cumin seeds, fennel seeds, cloves, cardamom pods, bay leaves or curry leaves and cinnamon sticks. Stir and cook until spices emit a fragrance. Approximately 30 secs to a minute.
3) Add the onions and cook until caramelized or golden brown 6-8 minutes. Add the tomatoes and cook for a few minutes longer.
4) Over medium heat, add the lamb marinade along with its sauce and cook, stirring occasionally until yogurt is absorbed by the lamb and the ghee is starting to separate from the meat, about 15-10 minutes.
5) Stir in the chilies and stir the mixture to make sure the lamb pieces get coated with the paste. Pour 1 cup of water and stir once or twice to deglaze the skillet. Bring the mixture to boil. Reduce the heat, cover the pan and simmer, stirring occasionally to prevent the curry from sticking to the bottom.
6) Cook until the lamb is cooked through and tender, approximately 20-25 minutes.

Pairs well with – Naan or with steamed Basmati rice

33.   Butter Chicken

This creamy chicken dish is popular among the mainstream Indian restaurants around the world. It hails from the northern part of India where cream and tomato are commonly used in dishes to achieve a tangy and creamy balance.

Serves 4-6 people

Ingredients:
1 ½ cups full-fat Greek yogurt
2 tbsp lemon juice
2 tbsp ground turmeric
1 tsp coriander powder
½ tsp ground black pepper
1 tsp cayenne
½ tsp ground cardamom
2 tbsp ground cumin
3 lbs chicken thighs, bone-in
1 stick unsalted butter
5 tsp oil (neutral in flavor like canola)
2 medium-sized yellow onions, peeled and diced
4 cloves garlic, peeled and minced
3 tbsp fresh ginger, peeled and grated or finely diced
1 tbsp cumin seeds

1 cinnamon stick
3 medium-sized tomatoes, diced
2 spicy chilies such as serrano or jalapeno or Anaheim, diced
1 ½ tsp, salt to taste
1 ½ cups cream
2/3 cups water
3 tbsp almond meal or almonds finely chopped
8 oz fresh or frozen peas
Handful of fresh cilantro, chopped with stems removed

Method:
1) In a medium-sized bowl, create a sauce by adding yogurt, lemon juice, turmeric, coriander, black pepper, cayenne, cardamom and cumin. Add chicken and with your hands coat to cover the chicken thighs. Refrigerate the chicken in a container with a cover overnight or for at least 4 hours.
2) On the day of cooking, heat a large pan over medium high heat. Add the oil and let it heat for a few minutes. Add butter and cook until it starts to foam. Add the onions, stirring frequently. Cook until translucent and slightly caramelized. Add garlic, ginger and cumin seeds and cook until the onions start to become golden brown.
3) Add the cinnamon stick, tomatoes, chilies and salt to the mixture and continue to cook stirring frequently. Add peas and water and bring the mixture to a boil, then lower the heat and simmer uncovered for 25 to 30 minutes.
4) Stir in the cream and simmer for an additional 10 to 15 minutes., until the chicken is cooked through.
5) Add the almond meal or chopped almonds and cook for 5 minutes longer. Remove from the heat and garnish with fresh chopped cilantro.

Pairs well with – Wonderful on its own or with steamed Basmati rice

34.　Sri Lankan Style Egg Curry

Many variations of egg curries abound, this one uses coconut milk, a signature ingredient found in Sri Lankan dishes to add a certain silky creaminess to the overall curry experience.

Serves 4-6 people

Ingredients:
4 hard-boiled eggs
2 tbsp coconut oil
1/2 tsp fenugreek seeds
¼ tsp mustard seeds
1or 2 cinnamon stick
1 medium onion, finely chopped
1-2 bay leaves
2 cloves
1 sprig curry leaves
1 to 2 green chilies
2-inh knob of fresh ginger, peeled and grated into paste
3 to4 cloves of garlic, smashed
1 can (13.5 oz) unsweetened coconut milk
1 tsp salt
1 tsp ground turmeric

Method:
1) Over a medium-high heat, heat coconut oil in a saucepan with wide-bottom. Add fenugreek seeds, mustard seeds, cinnamon stick. Cover the pan to allow for the mustard seeds to stop popping, for 30 seconds to a minute. Add the onions, bay leaves, cloves, curry leaves, chilies, ginger and garlic, cook for 5 to 10 minutes or until the onions become caramelized and appear golden brown in color.
2) Add the coconut milk, salt and turmeric to mixture. Stir to combine and bring the flavors together.

3) Gently add the eggs and simmer the curry uncovered, pouring the sauce over the eggs to cover and allow the eggs to bathe in its flavors.
4) Simmer on low heat until the sauce thickens for 10-12 minutes.

Pairs well with – any variation of flatbreads or with steamed Basmati rice

35.   Beef Vindaloo (Curried Beef Stew with Vinegar)

This is a goan inspired beef stew which uses the unusual combination of malt vinegar and coconut milk to balance out the tartness and add creaminess.

Serves 6-8 people

Ingredients:
1 lb boneless beef chunks, cut into 1-inch cubes
1 tsp cayenne or red pepper
3/4 tsp turmeric, ground
4 to 5 Yukon gold potatoes, peeled, cut into 1-inch cubes, submerged into cold water to prevent browning
3 tbsp coconut oil
3 to 4 cardamom pods
2 fresh bay leaves
1 cinnamon stick
1 medium onion, diced
2 tsp ground cumin
3 tsp ground coriander
1 can unsweetened coconut milk
2 medium tomatoes, diced
¼ cup apple cider vinegar

2 tsp kosher salt
Fresh cilantro, chopped for garnish

Method:
1) Prepare the beef the night before by marinating it in turmeric and pepper. Cover the bowl and refrigerate it overnight.
2) In a skillet over medium high heat, add the oil and allow it to get heated. Add cardamom, cinnamon, bay leaves and cook until the spices are aromatic. Add the onions and cook until golden brown or caramelized. Toss in the beef and potatoes. Continue to stir fry for 5-10 minutes.
3) Add cumin and coriander powder over the mixture and stir-fry for 2 more minutes.
4) Add the coconut oil, tomatoes, vinegar and salt. Stir to deglaze the skillet and allow the flavors to come together.
5) Raise the heat and bring the mixture to a boil, reduce the heat, cover and cook simmering the stew for 1 ½ hours or until the beef cubes turn very tender.

Pairs well with – any variation of flatbreads or with steamed Basmati rice.

Curry Accompaniments

36.   Curd Rice

This cooling rice dish is popular in southern parts of India. It is a very comforting dish to serve on a Friday night when you are winding down from a busy week and need some comfort as you approach the weekend.

Serves 6 people

Ingredients:
1 cup white Basmati rice or long-grain Jasmine rice, rinsed thoroughly
1 tsp salt
2 cups water

Tempering:
3 tbsp sesame or coconut or olive oil
1 tsp black mustard seeds
1 tbsp finely chopped ginger
3-4 whole dried red chilies
1 tsp salt
2 cups plain whole Greek-style yogurt

Method:
1) Prepare the rice by bringing the rice to a boil with water and salt, in a medium pot. Lower the heat, cover the pot and cook the rice until rice grains are cooked and tender – approx. 12 – 15 minutes.
2) While the rice is cooking prepare the tempering, by heating the oil in a skillet over medium high heat. Add the mustard seeds, cover the skillet and wait for 30 seconds for mustard seeds to finish popping. Add ginger, chilies and cook, stirring, for 1 minute. Add yogurt and salt. Stir and remove from the heat.
3) Combine the rice mixture with the yogurt mixture. Serve warm or at room temperature.

Pairs well with – Carrot or Lime Pickle

37. Pulao or Perfumed Basmati Rice

This is a basic rice recipe that uses cardamom and bay leaves to provide fragrance to the basic rice used to serve alongside curries.

Serves 6 people

Ingredients:
1 cup white Basmati rice or long-grain Jasmine rice, rinsed thoroughly
2 tsp ghee or butter
4-5 cardamom pods crushed
2 fresh or dried bay leaves
2 cups water
1 ½ tsp salt

Method:
1) In a medium saucepan, heat the ghee or butter over medium-high heat. Add the cardamom and bay leaves and cook for 30 seconds to a minute.
2) Add the rice, water, salt and bring the mixture to a boil. Lower the heat, cover and cook for 15 to 18 minutes or until the rice is cooked through and tender.
3) Turn off the heat and let it simmer covered for 5 to 10 minutes.

Pairs well with – any form of curries

38. Lemon Rice

Rice is staple grain of southern regions of India. Where the north relies on the wheat to make chapattis and naan, the south is very creative when cooking rice. This variation is made with lemon and it is as delightful as it sounds.

Serves 4-6 people

Ingredients:
2 tbsp canola, olive, coconut oil
4 tbsp raw cashews
1 tsp urad dal
2 tsp channa dal
½ tsp mustard seeds
¼ tsp ground turmeric
2 dried red chilies
1 sprig curry leaves
1 lemon, zested and juiced
Pinch of asafetida or to taste
2 cups cooked basmati rice
1 ½ tsp salt

Method:
1) In a medium-sized saucepan, heat the oil.
2) Add cashews and sauté for 3-5 minutes until golden brown.
3) Add the urad dal followed by channa dal. Stir to combine. Cook for 2 -3 minutes.
4) Add the mustard seeds, cover the pan and allow it to sizzle and pop for 30 seconds to an hour.
5) Add turmeric, chilies, curry leaves followed by a pinch of asafetida. Stir and cook for 1 minute.
6) Add the cooked rice to the mixture and fold and combine to allow the flavors to meld together.

7) Add the lemon juice, zest and salt. Stir to combine.
8) Fluff the rice and serve.

Pairs well with – Curries

39.　Basmati rice cooked in Saffron

This is another variation of a basic rice recipe and uses saffron to add the yellow speckled flecks on the white bed of basmati rice.

Serves 4-6 people

Ingredients:
1 cup Indian Basmati rice, rinsed
1 ½ cup water
4 tbsp ghee or butter or oil of your choice
3/4 teaspoon saffron threads
3 tsp granulated sugar or jaggery
½ tsp salt

Method:

1) In a medium-sized saucepan, heat the ghee or butter or oil over medium-high heat.
2) Add rice and saffron. Stir to coat the rice with the butter or oil
3) Pour 1 ½ cups of water. Add the sugar and salt. Bring the mixture to simmer.
4) Cook uncovered for 8-10 minutes. Avoid stirring.
5) Lower the heat, cover the pot and cook on the lowest setting for 8 to 10 minutes.
6) Remove the rice from the heat. Keep it covered and let it continue to steam for 10-15 minutes.
7) Fluff the rice and serve.

Pairs well with – Curries

40.   Spiced Semolina (Upma)

This is a popular breakfast dish hailing from the southern part of India. Made with coarse semolina grain, it also makes for an ideal one pot meal for a quick, weeknight meal.

Serves 4-6 people

Ingredients:
1 cup coarse or medium ground semolina
4 tbsp oil of your choice, butter or ghee
1 tsp black mustard seeds
1 tsp cumin seeds
1 tsp moong dal
1 tsp urad dal
½ cup raw cashews or peanuts
1 medium onion, chopped
1-2 dried red chilies or fresh green chilies such as serrano or jalapeno
1 tbsp minced or fresh grated ginger
½ ground turmeric
1 sprig fresh curry leaves
2½ cups water
¾ tsp salt or to taste
Freshly chopped cilantro for garnish

Method:

1) Start by roasting semolina, stirring constantly on a low heat in a wide skillet. Roast until fragrant and appearance is light golden brown.

2) In a medium-sized saucepan, heat the ghee or butter or oil over medium-high heat.

3) Once the oil is hot, add mustard seeds, cumin seeds, moong dal and urad dal. Fry until it crackles.

4) Add peanuts or cashews and roast for 3 to 4 minutes.

5) Add onions to the mixture, sauté until translucent and caramelized, approximately 8 to 10 minutes.

6) Add the chilies, ginger, turmeric and curry leaves, cook for a few minutes.

7) Raise the heat, add the water and salt and bring the spice mixture to a boil.

8) Lower the heat to keep the water simmering and start adding the semolina slowly. Stir constantly to mix and combine to blend.

9) Cover and let the upma steam for a few minutes until all the water is absorbed. Once all the water is absorbed, let the upma steam for a few more minutes before fluffing it.

10) Sprinkle cilantro leaves and serve warm.

Pairs well with – Curries

41.   Basic Bread (Roti)

Here is a basic version of a wheat based flat bread that is a staple among the households in India. You can choose to omit the baking powder if you like, the results will not vary by much.

Serves 4-6 people

Ingredients:
2 cups whole wheat flour (or combination of whole wheat and rye)
2 – 4 tsp oil, butter or ghee, melted, your choice
½ tsp baking powder
Salt to taste
¾ cup warm water

Method:

1) In a large mixing bowl add the flour. Make a well in the center and add oil, ghee or butter.
2) Rub the flour with the oil, ghee or butter. Add salt, baking powder and stir to combine.
3) Adding water in batches, start bringing the dough together.
4) Once the dough comes together, stop adding the water and start kneading it for 3 to 5 minutes.
5) The dough will be sticky, but should not stick to the finger.
6) Add the kneaded dough back to the bowl and make indents with your finger. Add some water. Cover the bowl and let the dough rest for a minimum of 30 minutes.
7) When ready to make rotis, grease your hands and ready some dusting flour on the side.
8) Make ball the size of a golf ball or smaller.
9) Roll it in the flour and bring to the rolling surface. Roll the ball out into a flat circle with the thickness consistency of your desire. Make sure it is not too thick or thin.

10) Heat a cast iron skillet over high heat. Once heated, add the rolled-out roti. With a spatula, spread some oil over the roti and cook until the top starts getting bubbly.

11) Flip the roti and cook the other side by spreading some oil on that side. Cook until the roti appears to start forming some golden-brown dots on top. Remove and proceed with the next one.

12) The first roti may take longer than the other. But once the stove griddle is hot, the rotis will cook fast.

Pairs well with – Curries

42. Fresh Corn Roti

This roti is reminiscent of the traditional roti from the Northern region of Punjab called 'Makki di roti' which is made out of corn flour. Here fresh corn is used with whole wheat flour.

Makes 16 Breads

Ingredients:
1 16 oz of frozen cut corn kernels defrosted or 2 cups fresh corn
2 cups whole wheat flour
½ tsp salt
1-2 tsp oil of your choice
Melted ghee or butter for brushing

Method:
1) Begin with pureeing the corn in a food processor with salt. Transfer to a mixing bowl.
2) Sprinkle whole wheat flour in batches until the dough comes together in a ball.
3) Knead a few times, the dough will be sticky, pour oil and coat the dough to prevent from sticking.
4) Cover and let the dough rest for 15 to 20 minutes.
5) Return to the dough when ready to prepare the rotis. Divide the dough in 16 equal portions by pinching the dough into smaller balls. Have extra whole wheat flour ready for rolling the dough to prevent sticking.
6) Heat a cast-iron griddle over medium-high heat.
7) Roll out the first roti, dust with the flour as necessary if the roti starts sticking to the surface. Add it to the pan. The first roti will take longer to cook than the remaining as the pan will get progressively hot.

8) Cook each side until cooked thoroughly. The first one will take a few minutes longer than the remaining.
9) As the pan gets warmed up, it will take approx. 1 min to cook each side.

Pairs well with – Delicious on its own or served with any of the curries

43.   Fennel Speckled Sweet Roti

A mildly sweet roti with fennel flavor. A little more butter or ghee is used here to provide more flakiness.

Makes 10 Breads

Ingredients:
3 cups whole wheat flour, additional for dusting
1 tbsp fennel toasted and coarsely ground
½ cup ghee or butter melted
1 cup warm water
½ cup brown sugar

Method:
1) In a large mixing bowl, add the whole wheat flour and sprinkle with ground fennel.
2) Add 4 tbsp ghee and rub the flour to mix.
3) Add ½ cup of the water and work it into flour mixture. Add small amounts of water as necessary and continue to knead the flour until it comes together.
4) Once the dough comes together, place it on the kneading surface by dusting with flour.
5) Rub hands with ghee and start kneading the dough. Knead the dough for 10 minutes until the surface is smooth and the dough springs back when poked with your finger tip.
6) Cover and let the dough rest at room temperature for 30 minutes.
7) Return to the bowl and divide the dough into 10 equal pieces.
8) When ready to cook, heat cast iron skillet over medium-high. Roll out the first ball half-way through, brush with ghee or butter and add a few pinches of sugar.

9) Pinch to enclose the sugar and form into a ball. Dust the dough ball with flour and roll out to approx. 7-inch round.

10) Add the rolled-out roti on the pan and cook on one side, flip and cook on the other side. Cooking time varies but shouldn't be more than 1 ½ minutes on each side.

11) A minute before the roti is cooked and you are ready to remove it off the pan, pour 1 tsp of ghee around the edge of the bread to let it fry for 1 additional minute.

12) Remove from the pan and repeat with the rest.

Pairs well with – Delicious on its own or served with any of the curries

44. Fresh Turmeric and Carrot Pickle

This pickle is popular in the northern states of India such as Gujarat and Punjab. They compliment the cream based curries of northern India. Their tangy and slightly salty taste makes them ideal for serving with flatbreads or alongside a meal.

Makes 16 oz jar

Ingredients:
2-3 medium sized carrots
1/4 cup fresh turmeric
1 tbsp kosher salt, or to taste
4 tbsp yellow mustard seed powder
Juice of 1 lemon

Method:
1) Prepare the carrots by rinsing them under cold water, scraping the top skin off with a peeler and set in cold water and proceed to do the same with the remaining 1 or 2 carrots.
2) Prepare the turmeric by doing the same, rinsing in cold water and peeling the skin. Add them into the water with carrots.
3) Cut the carrots into 3-inch-long sticks.
4) In a medium-sized mixing bowl, add the carrots and turmeric and sprinkle with salt, mustard powder and toss to combine.
5) Squeeze the juice of lemon over the contents of the bowl and toss to combine. Taste and adjust the salt.
6) Loosely cover the bowl and let it marinate at room temperature for 4 to 8 hours.
7) Transfer to a jar and refrigerate for up to a week.

Pairs well with – Delicious on its own or served with any of the curries

45.   Lime or Lemon Pickle

This pickle will take some time and patience, you will also need to gather some spices to add the zing, but it is well worth the wait and the effort. This type of pickle is a flavor bomb as it is packed full of tangy, sweet, spicy and savory flavors all combined into one.

Makes 32 oz or a quart

Ingredients:
12 limes or lemons, key limes ideal
1 medium red onion
1 serrano chili
1-1 ½ inch fresh ginger knob, peeled
¼ lb golden raisins
1 tsp cardamom seeds
1 tbsp black pepper
1 tbsp coriander seeds
1 tbsp mustard seeds
4 dry red chilies
1 ½ cup apple cider vinegar
3 tbsp kosher salt
1 cup (1/2 lb) brown sugar

Method:

1) Prepare the lemons or limes first by cutting in half. You will obtain 24 halves. In a food processor, add the 18 halves. With the remaining 6, extract the juice and discard.

2) Add onion, serrano chili, ginger, raisins to the lemons or limes in the food processor.

3) Process until minced and remove the mixture in a glass or ceramic bowl.

4) Next prepare the spices by gently roasting them on high heat. On a small skillet add the cardamom, peppercorns, coriander seeds and mustards seeds. Roast the spices for about 2-3 minutes. Remove from heat and let it cool.

5) Grind the spices once cool into a fine powder.

6) Add the ground spices, the juice of the limes, and the vinegar to the minced mixture and mix well. Cover and let the mixture marinate for 24 to 48 hours.

7) After the marination is complete, cook the lime or lemon mixture on a non-metallic pan over low heat. Add the salt and sugar. Continue to cook over low heat, uncovered for 30 minutes. Have 2 pint jars or one quart jar ready to pour the lime pickle into.

8) Remove from the heat, let it cool slightly and pour into a jar or jars. Seal and let it rest for at least 2 weeks before serving.

9) Once opened, store in the refrigerator

Pairs well with – Nice served alongside a roti or chapatti for a simple meal

46.   Tomato Coconut Chutney

This chutney contains the signature southern Indian flavors of coconut, yogurt, mustard seeds and curry leaves. It comes together in a cinch and is refreshing on a hot summer day when tomatoes are in full season.

Makes 2 cups

Ingredients:
1 small or medium tomato
1 ½ cups fresh grated coconut
¼ plain yogurt
1 small serrano chili
½ tsp kosher salt, or to taste

For Tarka:
2 tbsp oil of your choice
¼ tsp black mustard seeds
1 sprig fresh curry leaves
1 tsp split urad dal

Method:
1) Start with processing the tomato, coconut, yogurt, chili and salt in a food processor. Taste and adjust the salt accordingly. Transfer to a bowl and set aside.
2) Next prepare for tarka by heating oil in a small skillet. When hot, add mustard seeds, curry leaves and urad dal. Let it sizzle for a few minutes. Remove from the heat and set aside to cool.
3) Combine the yogurt tomato mixture with the mustard seeds curry leaf mixture. Mix and serve at room temperature

Pairs well with – alongside any Indian meal

Curry Masala Blends

47.   Garam Masala

This is the most common blend of spices that is versatile and provides any dish with great flavor.

Makes ¼ cup

Ingredients:
1 stick of cinnamon
2 tbsp whole cumin seeds
2 ½ tbsp whole coriander seeds
1 Tsp black peppercorn
12 whole cloves
1 tsp freshly grated nutmeg
10 green cardamom buds

Method:

1) Roast the spices to extract the flavor over a small skillet on medium-high heat. Once the skillet is hot, reduce the heat to medium-low, add the spices and toast gently by occasionally swirling the pan to make sure that the spices are continuously moving. After about 2 minutes, the spices will start to release a strong aroma, at this point, remove from the heat and let the spices cool on the skillet.

2) Once spices are cooled completely, transfer the toasted spices to a small food processor or a coffee grinder dedicated to blending the spices. Grind the spices to a fine powder.

3) Store the spice mix in an airtight container in a dark place for up to six months.

Pairs well with – Key ingredient in flavoring various curries

48.   Balti Masala

This masala blend is used in northern Indian style cream curries.

Makes ¼ cup

Ingredients:
2 tbsp whole cumin seeds
2 tbsp whole coriander seeds
6 whole cloves
2 sticks of cinnamon
8 cardamom pods
1 tsp whole ajwain
1 tsp fennel seeds
½ tsp mustard seeds
½ tsp fenugreek seeds
1 tsp dried fenugreek leaves
1 sprig of fresh curry leaves

Method:
1) Roast the spices to extract the flavor over a small skillet, on medium-high heat. Once the skillet is hot, reduce the heat to medium-low, add the spices and toast gently by occasionally swirling the pan to make sure that the spices are continuously moving in the pan. After about 2 minutes, the spices will start releasing a strong aroma, at this point, remove from the heat and let the spices cool on the skillet.
2) Once spices are cooled completely, transfer the toasted spices to a small food processor or a coffee grinder dedicated to blend spices and grind the spices to a fine powder.
3) Store the spice mix in an airtight container in a dark place for up to six months.

Pairs well with – Chicken Balti

49. Punjabi Garam Masala

This is another variation of the garam masala with added complexity in the flavors such as: black cardamom pods, heat from the ginger powder and sweetness from the bay leaves.

Makes ¼ cup

Ingredients:
4 tbsp cumin seeds
4 tbsp coriander seeds
2 cinnamon sticks
10 whole black cloves
5 fresh or dried bay leaves
3 black cardamom pods
5 green cardamom pods
1 tsp black peppercorns
1 tsp dried ginger powder
½ tsp freshly grated nutmeg

Method:
1) Roast the spices to extract the flavor over a small skillet on medium-high heat. Once the skillet is hot, reduce the heat to medium-low and add the spices and toast gently by occasionally swirling the pan to make sure that the spices are continuously moving in the pan. After about 2 minutes, the spices will start releasing a strong aroma, at this point, remove from the heat and let the spices cool on the skillet.
2) Once spices are cooled completely, transfer the toasted spices to a small food processor or a coffee grinder dedicated to blend spices and grind the spices to a fine powder.
3) Store the spice mix in an airtight container, in a dark place for up to six months.

Pairs well with – Chicken Tikka Masala

50. Bin Bhuna Hua Garam Masala

This spice blend is an untoasted version of the garam masala.

Makes ¼ cup

Ingredients:

2 tbsp coriander seeds
1 tbsp cumin seeds
4 whole cloves
6 whole black peppercorns
5 whole cardamom pods
1 fresh or dried bay leaf
1 dried red chili

Method:
1) Keep the spices untoasted and transfer to a small food processor or a coffee grinder dedicated to blend spices and grind the spices to a fine powder.
2) Store the spice mix in an airtight container in a dark place for up to six months.

Pairs well with – Rogan Josh

Indian Tools & Utensils

Although not essential, it's always useful to have the correct utensils for your recipes, below is a list of the utensils that will greatly help and enhance the wonderful Indian dishes that you are now creating.

Be sure to take a look at the link to our blog beneath the table at the end of the list, which provides an image of the utensil and the recommended model.

Utensil	Description	Use
Chakla & Belan	Round, flat platform typically made of wood with a rolling pin.	For making breads and rolling dough
Chimta	Stainless steel tongs	For Roti, assists with flipping
Colander	A bowl shaped, stainless steel sieve with a base.	For draining liquid away from food.
Degchi or Pateela	Stainless steel, brass or aluminium bowl with large opening and narrow neck.	For hot cooking ensuring the steam remains within the bowl
Hamam–Dasta	Aluminium or brass pestle & mortar	For pounding

Handi	Brass cooking bowl with wide opening	For curries and many dishes.
Kadai	Aluminium frying pan with deep depth	For frying suitable dishes.
Masala Dani	Spice container capable of storing a collection of spices	For housing all dried spices.
Moulds	Hollow container of various sizes and shapes	For setting food into desired shapes.
Parat	Large stainless-steel dish	For dough
Pauni	Brass or steel perforated spoon.	For skimming
Tandoor	A large cooking pot	For baking, but modern versions can also be used for frying and grilling.
Tandoor sariyas	Rods used to move breads and rotis	For use with the Tandoor in order to place food.
Tawa	Flat pan made of iron	For cooking Chipatis
Thali	Stainless steel plate with compartments	For serving dishes

Conclusion

As you may have observed, each dish more or less has some sort of spice in it, the use of spices, fresh herbs and various aromatics is the foundation of Indian curries. It provides great flavor and not to mention the myriad of health benefits when including them in your dishes. You can start your spice pantry with the basic cumin, cardamom, turmeric and ginger and continue to build from there.

If you are not accustomed to making dal or eating lentils, try the yellow lentil or moong dal which has a mellow and creamy taste and is very pleasing to the palate. The tuvar dal will take some time to get accustomed to, but once you get the taste for the legume, chances are you may find moong dal pale in comparison.

You are welcome to add meat and vegetables to the dal or lentil curries as you start adapting the recipes to suit your needs. I hope this book provides you with a basis that you will continue to build upon and encourages your curiosity to learn more about Indian culture and food.

If you've enjoyed these curries, why not sample more fantastic vegetarian and meat curry recipes, with my dedicated vegetarian and meat-based curry recipe books:

Also visit **www.ffdrecipes.com** to receive free exclusive access to our World Recipes Club, giving you FREE best-selling book offers and recipe ideas, delivered to your inbox regularly.

Thank you.

Cooking Measurements & Conversions

Oven Temperature Conversions

Use the below table as a guide to establishing the correct temperatures when cooking, however please be aware that oven types and models and location of your kitchen can have an influence on temperature also.

°F	°C	Gas Mark	Explanation
275°F	140°C	1	cool
300°F	150°C	2	
325°F	170°C	3	very moderate
350°F	180°C	4	moderate
375°F	190°C	5	
400°F	200°C	6	moderately hot
425°F	220°C	7	hot
450°F	230°C	8	
475°F	240°C	9	very hot

US to Metric Corresponding Measures

Metric	Imperial
3 teaspoons	1 tablespoon
1 tablespoon	1/16 cup
2 tablespoons	1/8 cup
2 tablespoons + 2 teaspoons	1/6 cup
4 tablespoons	1/4 cup
5 tablespoons + 1 teaspoon	1/3 cup
6 tablespoons	3/8 cup
8 tablespoons	1/2 cup
10 tablespoons + 2 teaspoons	2/3 cup
12 tablespoons	3/4 cup
16 tablespoons	1 cup
48 teaspoons	1 cup

8 fluid ounces (fl oz)	1 cup
1 pint	2 cups
1 quart	2 pints
1 quart	4 cups
1 gallon (gal)	4 quarts
1 cubic centimeter (cc)	1 milliliter (ml)
2.54 centimeters (cm)	1 inch (in)
1 pound (lb)	16 ounces (oz)

Liquid to Volume

Metric	Imperial
15ml	1 tbsp
55 ml	2 fl oz
75 ml	3 fl oz
150 ml	5 fl oz (¼ pint)
275 ml	10 fl oz (½ pint)
570 ml	1 pint
725 ml	1 ¼ pints
1 litre	1 ¾ pints
1.2 litres	2 pints
1.5 litres	2½ pints
2.25 litres	4 pints

Weight Conversion

Metric	Imperial
10 g	½ oz
20 g	¾ oz
25 g	1 oz
40 g	1½ oz
50 g	2 oz
60 g	2½ oz
75 g	3 oz
110 g	4 oz
125 g	4½ oz
150 g	5 oz
175 g	6 oz
200 g	7 oz
225 g	8 oz
250 g	9 oz
275 g	10 oz

350 g	12 oz
450 g	1 lb
700 g	1 lb 8 oz
900 g	2 lb
1.35 kg	3 lb

G

Cooking Abbreviations

Abbreviation	Description
tsp	teaspoon
Tbsp	tablespoon
c	cup
pt	pint
qt	quart
gal	gallon
wt	weight
oz	ounce
lb	pound
g	gram
kg	kilogram
vol	volume
ml	milliliter
fl oz	fluid ounce

Printed in Great Britain
by Amazon

32414609R00066